The First Home Air After Absence

Annie Stenzel

ISBN: 978-1-945917-19-6

Printed in the United States of America

Cover Image: *Untitled*, 1960, watercolor on paper,
©Richard Diebenkorn Foundation
Author Photo: Laura Duldner

"Making other books jealous since 2004"

Big Table Publishing Company
Boston, MA
www.bigtablepublishing.com

Table of Contents

To the poets—past, present, and future—whose words
both anchor and carry me.

Chiding the muse

"Make it new." ~ Ezra Pound

The fact is, all those fancy ways of saying things
are gone, and we're obliged to sit like tailors
with our scissors and our shipboard needle
trying to make or mend an impossible garment.
Make it how? With these pickled tools, husks of hands
and stomped-on shards of old significance?

It's as though you hire an architect for your dandy
custom structure, but then the builder
tries to frame the place with 2 x 4s warped
from the desert sun, or torqued by standing
water, the wood so compromised the grain now spurns
the saw, forbids the very entrance of a nail.

But since I'm still dumbfounded by the capsized
starbowl of a winter night; still court the sweet
pain caused by drawing breath when lilac is in bloom,
I can't be daunted, even though the very threat of speech
obscures all miracles. You told us, make it new,

yet how, when Babel's weight has crushed
the juice from every syllable?
How, when the word "rose" no more evokes that
sense-rejoicing synthesis of petals and fragrance
than the word "I" denotes this being who struggles
with a suitcase of self sealed in an envelope of skin.

One

Diorama, minus a fourth dimension

Each habitat is set apart from its improbable neighbor
as though the miles that separate the outback from the tundra
are compressed within the walls of each Lucite cage.

No fear that any trace of the wirewood trees and wattle,
the emu and bustard in the foreground, pack of dingoes
hunched by the carcass of a kangaroo at the rear

will creep next door to disturb the sere landscape
where a snowy owl nests near saxifrage, indifferent
to the caribou, wary of a fox on the horizon.

But in the next diorama down, that man in a tule boat
with the wealth of fish at his feet can't ever reach
his village, though a hearth waits ready and half-clad children

play by a flickering flame. As you walk through the silent hall,
Vesuvius will never overtake the frantic mother
who races away from Pompeii with an infant clutched in her arms.

Sisyphus addresses his boon companion

Dearest boulder, I would recognize you anywhere: that dolomitic bump is where I first placed my hands last time we started out together...yesterday, it must have been. The morning dazzled me with hope. Do you remember how I sang as we began, you before me silent as always, me with my strength complete and head held high as we began to climb? We tried the southern route again, chosen because the light seemed to illuminate the simplest path for our ascent. With the grade still gentle, it was delightful moving up and up and up with you over familiar ground, navigating gracefully every rut and hillock in our path.

You're less affected by the weather's pranks than I—rain, ice, fierce winds against your back; it's all the same to you—but wasn't yesterday a beauty, in its cold, solstitial way. Give me winter anytime, when I have heavy work to do.

Do you suppose I'll ever be accustomed to the singular moment that arrives each day, when my strength is nearly sapped from our long time upon the mountain, when I have done my utmost to position you strategically so that gravity won't undo our difficult accomplishment, when your indomitable fate frees you, right at the summit, from my pushing hands, and you dash off without me, down to where the day began?

Cassandra talks in her sleep

But if you're waiting for me
to Say things the way I used to
say things, don't bother.

There's no demand
for plangent images
from a soothsayer you won't hear

and not everything a seer says
is prophecy. As much as half
might be a plea for different weather

or a rumination on petulance
in the marketplace
and the price of peace.

Even so, sharpened pencils roll around
on the table, waiting; brushes
stand ready in the jar.

Aubade, in the eighth year of solitude

When far more than half the bed is chilly in the morning

When the winter nights are patches of sleep
on a fabric of restlessness

When the dark is not quite solid but
resembles pitch, in that it sticks
both when the eyes are closed and open

When, in my tiny abode, a glimpse through the open
bedroom door leads to the window
beyond which in daylight looms a view, rented
but much beloved, of bay, of sky, a bridge, a distant city

When I think of my many nights' companions—those
of long duration, or of little—think of the truths
and lies that mingled, caught in the sheets
when the words whispered from one
mouth or the other were heard, misheard, or ignored

When, racing through the corridors of my unstilled
mind I meet my old selves and the woman I always wished
I could be, and you all scold me for my faults,
berate me for the scolding, taunt me with mirrors broken
or whole, point at me and make shrill noises
in a language I don't speak

Then, at whatever hour is faithful to its season, as morning
slides its colors into place, reproves the sepia hues
that were credible until they were subsumed in pink
or violet, yellow, maybe even green on the horizon—
it really is a rosy-fingered dawn that circles
into place, rescues those of us who take our night-
times hard, and slips an innocent day onto the table

Order: Lepidoptera

A moth reminds me of myself
sometimes.
You know, the way a moth may
blunder here,
            blunder there,
blunder back again—
full of anxious purpose but
still aimless, somehow.

There was one on the 5:14 the other day, for instance,
and it made its bumbling way
three times the length of the bleak,
fluorescent light that bisects the bus, bumping its improbable body
on the roof, the light,
            the roof,
the back of the head of a person standing in the aisle,
the roof again.

So where does a moth think it's going, anyway?

"Somebody loves us all"

On the train with us this evening:
unspeakable stench.
You really can't imagine.
He sat alone, with empty seats
on either side and opposite.

No one could endure proximity
and this a rush-hour crowded train
packed end to end with suits
and dresses, coiffeur, clothing, skin all
scrupulously fragrant.

Positioned near the door, oblivious
to all eyes fixed on his amazing rags
this fellow went about his business:
from a dozen motley pockets he plucked
miscellaneous debris, examined
each specimen gravely,
then dropped it to the floor.

As the train, with its accustomed fanfare
left grateful passengers at station after station
the heap of items grew between his feet—
the near-bare feet with all those sores—

and it was odd to see the leaves,
the bits of moss, the feather, scrap
of redwood bark, a well-scrubbed wishbone
all lying on the grubby surface; as though
a portion of the forest floor had fled the city
and was speeding through the suburbs, headed home.

Parallel Lines

"… a region of space the size of a pea would be stretched larger than the observable universe in a time interval so short that the blink of an eye would overestimate it by a factor larger than a million billion billion billion." ~ Brian Greene

In my other life, I am contented
The days unfurl with elegant simplicity
Morning smoothes a path toward nightfall
If there is no ecstasy, at least there is no dismay

As the days unfurl with elegant simplicity
this is one universe; countless others may exist
If ecstasy is absent, neither is there dismay
I have yet to meet any of my Doppelgänger

This is our universe; many others may exist
We could all be replicated to the last detail
No sign as yet of any Doppelgänger
Same soul, same work, same avocation

We all could be replicated in every detail
Plenty of time and space—infinite, actually
Same work, same soul, same avocation
We all probably cry when we hear Schubert Lieder

Plenty of space and time—infinite, of course
Shoulder to shoulder but completely invisible
We probably all cry over Schubert Lieder
How ingenious that the molecules manage so well

Shoulder to shoulder but totally invisible
One existence per lifetime—must that be so?
Ingenious that the molecules manage so well
Each being persuaded of his or her own uniqueness

One lifetime per existence—is that really true?
Morning smooths the path toward nightfall
Each being persuaded of her or his own uniqueness
I am contented, in my other life

I leave the Iron Age entirely to one side

The Stone Age makes sense.
So little time; so many enemies;
a world of want, *if* you survive

your infancy. You take a stone,
shape it with another stone, affix it to a
branch with supple vine:
here's a weapon, blunt and brutal.

But the Bronze Age baffles:
your campfire wasn't nearly hot enough
to smelt the tin by serendipity.

Wide vein of copper in a rock?
A pretty thing, and I can see you
pick it up, transport it home

and talk it over with your people.
But was it happenchance
that chunk of stone landed in the kiln?

Was it when you first saw molten
copper, watched it harden, held its bright
potential in your hands, struck it
with your trusty stone-made hammer,
took in the texture's change?

Was that when time contracted and you raced
headlong to sword, shield, and spear, arrow
tip, dagger, battle axe—your dazzling armory?

Odd: Job

Is it too late now for me to try my hand
as an eppler welter, a pluma skiver
a fig caprifier, or an aitchbone breaker?

It never occurred to me when I was young
to be a slubber doffer or a bridge tender
a chow-chow maker or a cicerone.

Why did I never think of punching the clock as
drag-sawyer or a fox-lathe operator
a hot-stone setter or a lay-out girl?

And I never saw an ad for a thimblerigger
or had a chum who loved
working all those years as a weirkeeper.

But I did as child feel pretty certain
I'd be a great funambulist and
okay on the trapeze.

Who'd have thought I'd spend
a lifetime doing all sorts of other
odd jobs instead. Including this one.

Cronos: his tempo

Back in the day, a traveler
on a dusty road might say to a person
in the town along the way

What news?

And whatever news was vital
passed from one to the other
then, thirst or hunger slaked,

the traveler headed on
along the necessary path
until the next encounter; the next

What news?

News had to travel at a walking pace
not, as it does in our agitated era
at the speed of sparks along a wire—

as though traveler and bystander
were positioned always each
within the sound of the other's voice

never mind the miles and thoughtful days
that used to separate them
from the tidings' conveyance

so that catastrophe, no matter how
extreme, was already cushioned
by time's quiet pillow

before someone, perhaps at my remove
learned of it at last
and fell to pieces.

Walking in Lines with Five Feet

What have we to say that bears repeating?
Statements that start out *I love* ... or *I'm sorry* ...
those are best. The rest of speech will mostly
miss the mark we aim for. Language frets free

the instant syllables escape the lips:
so little mercy from our mouths. Wonder
is best expressed in music, or in clay,
unless the gods send motes of meaning, blessed

by truth and beauty, to a skillful hand,
and then that hand moves without fear across
the snowy page. Scant are the essential
writings from our kind. Clouds are more fluent.

Oceans can't go wrong, inscribing endless
hieroglyphics the sand does not ignore.

All of it, and Spring as well

When I have thought of your
long torso, sloping
thighs, the cake-like taste of that
wide space below your shoulder

and rocked back on my heels
from memory of the tone you
say my name in, your face turned sideways,
your hands locked in my hair almost too hard,

if it is morning, early, and the birds
are frantic from the sun around the sprinklers,
and on the air from elsewhere
comes some fecund scent of Spring

I must sit down, abruptly,
close my eyes against the weakness
in my ankles, in my elbows,

calm my breathing with the thought that
you are not, not yet,
(not quite) too much for me.

"Fall down seven times, stand up eight"

Sometimes, disappointment hits me with both barrels
and the near-tears stand fierce on eye-brims and it's hard
to remember my mantra, a proverb, some pithy
quotation I found about what Churchill used to say.

Sometimes you spend all day trying: stack
the blue block on a red block, then another,
and another, 'til your tower scrapes the sky
for one brief moment. Then a bully knocks it down.

Sometimes the Fates will be severe upon me
mile after mile as I plod along with my hands
full, no place to put my burden down even though
I'd like to remove a tiny pebble from my shoe.

Sometimes you're just sure you've built a better
mouse-trap, discovered El Dorado, found the missing link,
written a best-seller, rescued a princess from
the fiercest of all dragons. And then you wake up.

Sometimes, the daily grind is not that trendy
coffee flavor but the lowest sandpaper grit grade
I can find at the hardware store, ruthlessly
applied to my tenderest surfaces. All day long.

But sometimes beauty rushes toward you as though
propelled from a hard-to-hold fire hose
and the joy is just too, too much, but
you still have to keep your eyes open. I do.

But we are really the dust of ancient stars

The difference between immigrants
and natives
is all in your mind.
Nobody got here first.
We all crawled out
of the womb together
and even that was not the beginning.

Whether you believe in Eve, or evolution,
you must know our ancestors
share a common grave.
Everyone's blood is blue
while safely contained
in the body
and then, when shed,
always bright red.

Two

The garden came first

"Eve was framed." ~ bumper sticker

Perhaps she was already
weeding. You know how it is:

step into the yard
for a moment because

you hear birdsong
then glance

down at the ground and see
weeds

everywhere. You have to do
something, which means

you have to decide:
oxalis or chamomile?

vinca or Bermuda grass?
dandelion or morning glory?

So, which one was put here
on purpose?

Another April, moderately cruel

In Japan, at Ashikaga, pilgrims
circle a wisteria planted
when Meiji was ruler.
Now it covers half an acre.

Here, you can't help but falter
then approach the drooping clusters
(pink or white or vaguely purple)
as they cascade toward the ground.

You have to plunge your face
into that delicate effusion
with its fragrance of times past—a scent
that some call cloying, some, sublime.

Wherever confronted with wisteria
you must stop and note a presence;
all this attached to wrist-thick branches that
can throttle a maple, creep up the roofline

or pull your house from its foundation, too.

Truth or dare

Truth is, I want to know you as a glove
knows hands (knows the one from fitting
onto it, the other, nestling into it); want
to know you as the senses know the first
home air after absence (find some faint
rose-hint and an old book memory in a room
where hardly anything has changed)

A Brief Natural History of the Sub-Continent

How long can it be that you fascinate me the way
mongoose eyes cobra? What happens when what is savage
within everyone finds its egress from one of us—or both:

from your hooded eyes; from my narrowing lips.
Does a cobra need venom? Can a mongoose kill
using pure fury? What is secreted when born

enemies meet has a scent, or a texture known somehow
to each. Here, it is confusing. Am I mistaking this acrid taste,
fresh from my fingers, for fear?

Could it be that your instinct, strong from its long
reign, is the real traitor? About cobra and mongoose:
when they fight to the death, don't they sometimes both win?

Grow sorrow

"Time to plant tears, says the almanac." ~ Elizabeth Bishop

Our garden book says nothing about salt
and nicotiana—whether the latter objects to the former

      my hands in the earth slowly shifting
      worms as they writhe in the sudden light

all through the yard, pockets of odd debris
still surface to surprise us: strips of tar paper, glass, bent nails

      knees bare on the green pad
      move inch by inch along the little bed

six crimson-flowered plants, a trowel's length apart
the salt distributed drop by drop

Hydra of the many names

(An argument)

always mindful
you will never
win one battle

        who could not love
        Bermuda buttercup or
        African wood-sorrel?

let alone the war
with oxalis
you must seize

        what's not to admire
        about Goat's foot, or
        even Soursop?

every opportunity
to pull up flower,
root, and bulb

        and the Latin name –
        oxalis pes-caprae –
        don't you think

or you will find
the whole yard
strangled:

        that has the ring
        of something
        you might find
        beautiful?

a yellow scream
that even Hercules
would fear

Late summer, lasting

That September when the long heat made you whisper "I surrender" through your teeth for hours every night and all the corners of the house were tried for sleep crimes, each side arguing its own complaint—you were out of bed a dozen restless times; the air too still unless the fan was on, the fan a raucous buzz, thanks to the balance of the blade you mended hastily two years ago. Past midnight, past 1:20, past 2:55, you can't help but see each dim-lit digit flicking past unslept-through. You get up, then down, up, down, a venture to the couch short-lived (the clammy skin says No to the cushion's texture); the bed intolerable after several minutes spraddled prone and damp across the bottom sheet. Your place is small, and these rooms shrink with every passing hour. There is a small yard out the back door and it is cooler there, much cooler. You try the last lounge chair still outside, struggle to fix it semi-horizontal; recline about 10 minutes before sensing Creatures stealthy in the shadows—skunk? raccoon? opossum? In the suburb: certainly it might be one of these, but likeliest a neighbor's cat. Waver, argue silently with apprehension, recognize the customary bugs at least have sensed your presence, retreat to the mock security indoors. After so much living in a dozen fascinating places, you have memories galore to keep you company but they did not content you those September nights. What is the point of casting your mind back to other nights you hoped would never end (you loved them so) when you're desperate for oblivion, even though infinite sleep creeps closer all the time.

Vinculum

"Only connect! . . . Live in fragments no longer." ~ E.M. Forster

Only connect? Whatever that entails
your efforts will be unavailing.
Try again, round peg:
Square hole—as usual.

A universal fact, though truly indigestible:
We strive and strive, but Zeno's paradox dictates
that each of us remain discrete, forever poised
at the uncrossable boundary between

self and someone else.

Provenance, as applied to a stone

Within days, perhaps hours, of your picking it up, a stone
is lost to its old home forever.

> Say goodbye to the stream-bed or the tide-pool, little rock:
> curiosity plucks it up; admiration holds it to the light;
> some superstition about what it might signify bears it away.

What becomes of the long-time custom of dropping into a pocket
those pieces of serpentine, sandstone or chert?

> Most of these treasures are ditched
> at the motel door once it turns out
> color flees them when they dry.

And yet: today, in my mother's cut-glass bowl—
the one I rarely use, that in her day held rhubarb
or cranberries for a holiday meal—put the stones there
and see the wild congregation of yellow and grey, white, green

> and black, the round, the rough, the smooth?
> Just add water, and wherever they came from
> surely the stones will remember.

If bees are few

for Emily Dickinson

To write at all
is the hardly
possible thing, and yet
one says, just
as you did to
your antique-
modern self: Yes, *write*.

Wondering
and wanting
to know—to be
told it was vital;
would survive
the years in drawers;
arrive in print
and stay—do you
know now?

To write what might
endure, absorbed
in heads, by heart—
recited in and
out-of-doors
after great pain—

Today, to know,
to believe firmly
what is necessary
to be written:

if you can,
you must—
if you must,
you do.

Seasoned

The light in late November wears
its winter face, even at this latitude:

long shadows and everything a little
pallid; the sun skulking around

a few degrees above the horizon, even
though its heat is more than ample

for so late in the year. Great fires
are in the news again, or still; we fret

about the lack of rain, no snowfall
yet—what will become of the ski-fields.

People have pulled warm clothes out of moth-
balls, whether they wear wool or not.

As the days get shorter we act a bit
ursine: eat more, draw the drapes by 5 p.m.

clutch morning covers close.
Tired season in our bones, we watch

a sunset's glory greedily; study the moon's
rise as tenderly as when we gaze at babies' faces.

In hospitals

when I am not the patient, I'm aware
of pain in its gauzy form;
the way it builds in rooms kept quiet.
As I watch you, pain keeps me
company (it keeps you captive)
it whispers at the walls, murmurs
around the furniture, moans from your
much sicker neighbor's bed.

While I am sitting vigil I almost
expect a foghorn's warning, a hollow sound
that makes pain more
than a monosyllable, that tolls
to tell me what depths pain has sunk to—
long, low notes announcing that
a mist of pain prevents our seeing far.

Perhaps I should not think it
odd that when I try to leave
your pain behind I find
it leaks from the doorway still, laps
at my feet while I wait
for the down elevator.

When you live in the city and dream

When you live in the city and dream of a farm
it's hard to parse the symbols; but you have to
ask why sleep summoned creatures from the barn,
field, or pond to bear a message. Why the laughable duck?
It's true you saw two mallards recently, huddled
beside a trail, but this dream-duck, domestic and solitary,
waddled beside a muddy pond,
sardonic tinge to its every quack.

Why, too, a pristine cow, when cleanliness
in a paddock is close to impossible? A bright,
impeccable Holstein, clearly iconic, but why does it stand
stage-right with a meditative gaze, chewing cud?
The pigs, at least, were dirty specimens,
there to remind you real vegetarians
make no exception for a B.L.T.

As for the heavyset horse, he must be there
to carry burdens back and forth without
complaint, the clip-clop from his hooves
like a lullaby, then the soft nicker of thanks when the oats arrive.
Only the chickens make sense: here and there
in urban areas, spotted out the window of your train
speckled hens may cross a tidy yard.

And the conversational quality your Kiwi sister imparts
to the chooks she feeds is so amusing: *ooh! tasty bugs
and tired lettuce bits, yum-yum. I'll give you an egg.*

It's true your history permits a throng of sheep to fill the view—
they entered from a distant country in another time,
so their significance is simple: that was your youth,
with all its charms and demerits, and now it's gone.
But what to make of the finale? Goats,
standing with their unkind eyes fixed on you
and they have just one word to say, over and over: *Saaad.*

The ache of lack: a play in words

For lack of a cornice, a mortise, a purpose
or just in want of solace, the solstice (more notice!)

who does not yearn for justice—a lattice
or perhaps merely a serviceable poultice?

You veer toward the precipice to practice
your sacrifice, but cowardice prevents you.

You need an accomplice, or at least
an apprentice to help stage your next caprice.

Once safe from the pious or pretentious
we'll drink from the sinuous chalice.

No need to be jealous of another's prowess—we can all
splash about safely right here in the deep serendipitous.

After walking meditation

Buddha leads me
to believe
I belong to
your trillion-piece puzzle
where this butterfly's mere
flutter has the force
of Hoover Dam

which is why
you must know: Fear
shackles my ankles. How
can I flee water
or wolves
with my feet
as fiercely bound
as an ancient
Chinese daughter's?

I do not make a good knight

Long time ago they put me in a suit of armor, shiny then and sure to be impervious. It was just like the ones they wore that kept them clean of blood, clanking safely from place to place. I was too tiny for my armor's size but as they said I would, I did grow into it. In time it fit, in fact felt snug and thus defended me against all comers. Some things did ding its surface, yes—left narrow scores on metal aging through the seasons. Other hazards lasered in through chinks and found soft tissue; marred major organs (but not in ways that could be felt or seen.) And yet the enemy long since has been on this side of the shield, keeping me close company. The armor cannot easily accommodate the size we are, the strength we've gained from our proximity. And one of us wants out. The other wants a new suit: metal made more supple so it drapes in graceful ways, becoming to a modern age. You've guessed the problem, doubtless: the hands that put the armor on can't help me take it off again. The rust that clots the joints has had long years and damp to fix it solidly in place. Stuck in this cramped and airless space I say, *I'm leaving*—beat my body back and forth against protection that became a cage. I say I'm leaving but I still don't go and my companion won't leave without me.

Three

Combustion

Every word of the next great work swirls
between the banks of almost any mind.

The notes, too, of a composition
whose melody will stir and endure

plus the colors on a canvas that will root your feet
to the ground in the gallery; open your eyes extra-wide.

So what stands between the notes, the words,
the brush strokes, and a world that waits with bated

breath for the next unforgettable? Only this ordinary
moment, crushed under the tread of sorry labors—

that, and the spark to ignite
an inextinguishable desire.

When a rainy morning starts out cryptic

Part-bug, part-fish, quite sizable, entirely scary
but not completely unexpected: this product
of a dream that followed insufficient sleep
scurried crazily across the floor while you all

watched in … should I call it consternation
or amusement? and I barked "find something
to contain it! but not that urn, for heaven's
sake—that isn't mine" whereupon some other

mutant creature with a large cockroach component
dashed out of concealment, began consuming
part-bug, part-fish (though they were roughly
the same size) and there endeth the message,

which I tell you now I do not even
wish to understand.

Stuck/Torn

"All change is for the worse." ~ Anon.

Because the fabric is tight-woven
like the bright sheets flapping
on the clothesline

    because the mingled contents
    of each kitchen drawer bespeak the lumbering years
    of meals prepared in tandem

        because the rut has earned
        its fame for comfort, being now furnished
        with every contemporary necessity

            because the yoke we wore as guardians
            of first, toddler, then, child, now, adolescent,
            binds us still in furrows across the same field

                because the drug of hope
                seduces and deceives
                with its diverting promises

                    because a cactus waits with patience
                    for the few but necessary drops
                    the rainy season will provide—

                        waits, parched in almost every cell

Sonnet for Constituents Not Permitted

"The syntagmatic relations which define the constituent
'he frightened' permit it to be followed by certain types
of constituent only: 'George', 'the man standing on
the corner', 'thirty-one field mice', etc.; but not 'the stone',
'sincerity', 'purple', 'in', etc." ~ Jonathan Culler

If it turns out you have to frighten
purple, or the stone, remember
as you do, this prohibition. Then
when at last the stone surrenders,

when you're compelled to hear its moan
of apprehension, if waiting field-mice,
empathetic, tremble on that lone
mineral's or hue's behalf, think twice

of de Saussure, and be aware
of his sage counsel, but
tell him it's not that hard to scare
a royal color. And tell him you know of a hut,

south-facing in the hundred-mile winds,
comprised of ten thousand terrified chunks of stone.

Angels be with us on transit

After the earthquake-interrupted night
morning limps forward, uninjured but frail:

> vignettes append to the dim shadows
> peopled with a frowning

crowd; with you, thick-lensed-glasses man
and you, crumple-cheek lady wearing shawl.

> Train noise insulates the otherwise-silent
> assembly. Everyone's head is bowed.

Plenty of time to count beards
and near-beards in this compartment.

> Stranger, we might love each other suddenly
> if we stopped with a shudder in the underwater

tunnel—power off and the lights gone out.
Some might snarl; some would quail;

> but some would surely gentle one another
> if the bough broke and the cradle fell down.

Hic sunt dracones

My offer to sleep without blankets
until you are warm
strikes you as odd. *Will you starve
when I'm hungry? Lie awake if I'm
restless?* you ask me. I scowl and nod.

That was the part of the dream
I held on to, and groped for my pen
to record in the dark. *My love
is not even: it's awkward*, I write
with a wavering hand. Someone sobs.

Rough times in this dream life:
the waters are wicked, the symbols
unclear. I play several roles.
Once I throttled myself
while I watched with great horror;

tried to cry *wait—I'm dangerous*
but no one could hear. Years ago
with a fever I strayed into rough country—
no map, no guide, but I got out
alive. Trouble is, now the place looks like

home when I wake up—and you?
I have no idea who you are.

Twelve lines of twelve syllables each

Say it's the fault of the rain, this pang that won't stop.
And yet, we needed rain, we wanted rain, we danced
to summon it, in bodies made out of water.

Desire is dangerous. We learn this young. If we
forget, we must start over, which is dangerous.
Far better to roll with Ouroboros, it's true.

To have kept too much is like having kept nothing:
as a forest, you see no trees. If a tree, no
forest. Now I belong to what belongs to me.

Say it's all hope's fault, regardless of the feathers:
our baby fingers reach up to clasp a sunbeam;
with our last syllables, we beg to see more light.

Sonnet for a master singer

Now that the mockingbird is back, our yard
is noisy in an ancient way. I love
the strident, tireless concert. I can't be bored
even when he makes alarm clock sounds above

the house. An urban type, he mimics some
he cannot possibly have ever heard.
A cardinal won't really come
this far west of the Mississippi.   I ask him, Bird,

(I call it "he" most of the time, though my
research suggests the female sings as well)
where in the world did you acquire
a repertoire with all those songs? The spell

you cast to claim my neighborhood as yours:
to sing the whole night through. I listen at all hours.

I mumble *deo gratias*
for Gerard Manley Hopkins

New light having touched tree-
tops, a line *there lives the dearest*
freshness fills my mind and I am
gladder still; another time the solid
roar of city shrieks my ear, I hear
seared with trade, bleared and panic
less. There is the slick
snail-track of freeway flat
on a hill—*man's smudge*—the stench
of new fuel at the gasoline
pump—*man's smell*—how well
you knew us, then and now.

But on a glory-day sometimes
with salt air or high pine
in my face, my spirits down around
my ankles even though *nature is never spent*
I think, full of fear, about *the last lights*
off the black west, wonder: is the soil
too bare? am I equal to my toil?
then, whole and true to my lips come
the *ah! bright wings* you gave the world.

In theory

"Bees, then, know just this fact which is of service
to themselves, that the hexagon is greater than the
square and the triangle and will hold more honey for
the same expenditure of material used in constructing
the different figures." ~ Pappus of Alexandria

Dreamless, but sleeping, she tucks the hours into parcels
at day's end, then stitches the selvage sides together:
fabric of memory to be basted into the necessary
garment of consciousness when she's awake.

Other nights are in the hands of edgier directors
and the sleeping state comprises different galaxies; matter
from every quadrant of the genome
it has cost the planet all this time to fathom.

We follow gravity by necessity, propelled from
that first aperture through the whirl of years
toward re-disintegration; the return
into component parts: our dust, now different dust.

Entire and distinct as we believe ourselves to be—our whole
experience homed (or simply housed) in material vessels—
we're mere geometry, shaped by the plod of evolution
out of our old freedom in space: as atom and atom, unknowing.

Vipassana practice

The teachings suggest:
avoid attachment. It is
the enemy of serenity.

Now I can see the Buddha's
ageless smile: there is nothing
certain but change. My love and I

stepped out of the place
where anything could happen.

The teachings suggest:
avoid attachment. It is
the enemy of serenity.

Something happened.

Hear that lonesome whistle blow

In the first months after the caboose
uncoupled from the crippled train, the quaint
car stood on the siding, grateful for relative peace.
Other traffic shook the ground it stood on
but the wheels were well-braced. Only the sides
trembled occasionally when the world hurtled past.

Then what? Seven years, that number rich in magic,
made their way past the solitary relic. Some crept,
others, for no obvious reason, moved at a dizzying
pace, covering the caboose in dust, rust, and forgetting.
This is year eight, in the East an auspicious number.
Did you notice a flicker of light behind one window?

Here are more to mourn

When it is your turn to suffer loss upon loss,
it's better to face forward. Stand square, griever.
Blink only when you must. Let pain
become your pulse, and then breathe in the gloom
of knowing that one is gone, and *that* one is long gone
and they are leaving one by one, as you will too.

Those who came before you knew, but
never could impart (save by example) the way
to scoop raw meaning from your heart
and serve it plain. No need to hold out
your best porcelain; just heap the trencher crust-high
with your daily fare of life and move along.

If you have courage to repeat the same word
here, then you're free to say three times
and more the word you need—to say, death, dead,
death again. Go on. Be bold, although the truth
remains unpopular: it's Comrade Death in his marching boots
who helps the world go on and on and on.

When I say "you," I mean all of us

There is no cure
for endurance. Either you can't or you do.
Hands up, supplicant;
hands down, triumphant.

Once you adjust
to the constant roar only catastrophe
could ever suppress,
you muddle along. By grace.

When in pain, wait.
When in doubt, don't.
This planet dangles
from the ear of the universe.

"The sea's off somewhere, doing nothing"

But day in and day out, it washes its shores, tithes
from one month's tide-drawn revelation, then another
never a day without the business of existence:
being water and salt. The seas are all off somewhere,
doing everything they can until the day comes
when there is nothing for them to do.

More than half the globe is condemned to eternal
restlessness, salt suspended in water, a body
held between uncertain boundaries, compelled
to pull by its power rocks into smooth, new
configurations, perpetual music tumbled together.

The planet's waters flow toward each other
but rarely touch: the Pacific might aspire
to quiet itself on a Mediterranean beach, but is thwarted.
The Arctic's true capacity is as uncertain as the lifespan
of those glaciers whose pace is no longer glacial—clumps
of old ice race toward the sea like lemmings.

On Witnessing the descent of Another into depression

When I say she has taken the veil
again, you might grieve for us both.
But it's really the veil that has taken her: as if a frail
vessel came under the hands of its least

skillful sailor just as it neared the lee
shore. Be afraid. There can be no
facile resolution. Think Demeter
but with no prospect of Persephone.

Balancing: the act

If you have ever watched a great funambulist
perhaps you can see her still, owning the air
below her without fear; walking a filament above the ring
the way other mortals saunter a street.

Then even if you only went to tightrope school
a time or two, decades ago
you'll always remember
the infinite wobble of the rope.

Impossible to imagine walking more than steps
on the long span. But there was one moment of glee
from every brief triumph, albeit closely followed
by gravity's jarring retort.

During your attempts to stay aloft
you were suspended perhaps two feet
above the floor of a cavernous hall in Paris
where a little circus had its winter home.

There, for a modest fee, you could watch
and learn, and, as your ankles trembled to support you
on the half-inch diameter cable you might receive a moment's
guidance if the guardian of the place saw merit in your try.

Baissez pas les yeux! he barks over and over, because
looking down is the kiss of death to your time on a tightrope.
So: no sparkling costumes for you. No oohs and ahhs
from a dazzled crowd. You just could not Not look down.

Umbrage

Autumn morning—how my shadow
    sometimes captures
        my attention—it must be
            that other slant of light

*un*certain and perhaps
    presages my winter—
        its afflictions; its oppression.
        Shadow, why are you

a stranger? Too thin to look much like me—
    a little hunched—not striding
        jauntily along as I do—and with
            your head at such a distance

from the rest of me.

Litany

Body of water before me, its edge
at my feet   I say to myself *Don't jump! Things will surely*
get better   Body of water before me, autumn
leaves in its shallows with tadpoles   A squiggle
of watery sun on the surface that barely
moves   no breath, no wind
Body of water before me of course
I won't jump; I have shoes
on   the sun a warm hand
at my shoulder   slight scent of the tree
Benjy said Caddy smelled like   but this isn't
a novel   Body of water before me
that tree a willow   in springtime will drag
lissome branches across
the body of water before me where
there is no disappearance from pain   into the body
of water before me   not a lake
or the sea   not river   pool   lagoon
just a small pond

Four

"Light travels at 300,000 kilometres per second"

Do you recall first learning that the world is round
and not just that, but spinning
wildly on its axis

and not just that, but this whole planet
merely one of several (and not even the largest!)
while the sun that seems so mighty a burning thing

would, from a distance, look as small and inconsequential
as a star does when seen in midnight's blue for the first
time, and the sky itself is but the most minute fraction

of a stunning nothingness (called Space) so comprehensive that the
whole endeavor—a small child's effort to understand
scale in the universe—has to be abandoned, once and for all.

Measure the dark

To measure the dark I will use a piano—
a grand piano gleaming black that waits
on stage to be played by four hands.

There was a sliver-moon above the flat
slab of empty ocean. So little moon
in a landscape without other light?

But I need a new way to talk about
the dark that filters out
onto a star-spun sky and there

lingers for anyone to remark: how
black the night, and big, and empty of all warm
features. You will tell me

there is a heat that lingers still
in stars icy only because distant; stars
that coruscate just as those in our eyes

are sometimes said to twinkle.
Here I must add: light-years create that effect
without intention. The flecks of light

just make the surrounding dark harder
to fathom. The space behind the closed eye
of a black cat is not that dark, nor even the inmost

region of a cave in the sub-continent where you stand
without a candle, your eyes straining
to open a little wider: that dark. Thus, a piano

playing Schubert—perhaps an Impromptu—
and rich notes will reach deep into the core
to plumb the nature of darkness itself

because even an opaque landscape
deserves exploration, and in the face of this desire
I fear nothing.

The warder of his brain

When my father died, his memory died with him.
That great repository of a million things is gone—
poetry in German, Italian, Greek; railway
schedules from three score years ago; dates

of anniversaries, birthdays of people whose very names
hardly anyone even remembered.
You could ask him, what does Papageno say
in the second act of Die Zauberflöte? Or

Churchill's comment about Gallipoli—how does that go?
Or items even more arcane and infinitely forgettable
like the year the transistor radio was invented. *Who cares?*
one might wonder (and occasionally we did) but now

the loss of that odd multitude
is part of the sorrow. Now no one else knows
what accounts for the quick frisson
each Fifth of October brings. And the amber brooch

I wear on the black wool jacket—who gave it to whom?
and why? Perhaps you will remind me how terrible
it might have been otherwise, had his memory
died before he did. And it's true: I do thank goodness

he escaped his sister's fate, the one who can't
remember where she is, who I am, or that she ever had
a brother who could quote the Bard
on any subject, by the hour.

Posture [im]Perfect

Bearing in mind the long hall of the tract home
you walked up and down with your sisters while Ma

watched gimlet-eyed and you three held your breaths
and stared raptly before you, heads fixed firmly

beneath whatever book you had chosen to balance—
two things are now sad, or three, on a good day:

what book did you carry? why can you no longer
walk with your head held high? and especially, why,

why did you never forgive your big sister before
her untimely death and actually not quite even then?

Present: Three Takes

"Where is it, this present? It has melted from our grasp."

~ William James

1

First, to have been born
human; then, not to have died on either of two
occasions when you were an inch
out of death's path: voilà, you are present.

2

Yesterday, as you strode along on a rich March morning,
your walk presented you with a trio
of hyacinths, two purple, one white.
To gain access to the light, they were shouldering
their way out of hard-packed earth adjacent
to the sidewalk beneath your feet.

3

Today you are making a gift for an unborn
baby, stitch by stitch coaxing a crib blanket
from 12 skeins of yarn. With every knit
and purl, you knot love into a coverlet
for a new being, and your pleasure
in this making is present enough.

"do not look directly into the light"

ripple marks and dark   shallow water,
muddy bottom   overlain by finer shale
extrusive, formed   so soils from serpentine
differ by the presence   columnar, very dark
of elements, the simplest   particles appear stretched
     greywacke   gabbro

brittle stars and crinoids   slow cooling, so obsidian
usually form a mounded   fracture along
economically important deposits
windows in stoves in the past   common, heavy, dark
     hemimorphite   hornblende

in shales of different   spectacular tufa
crystal shapes result   tumbled and carried
smooth-faced angular shapes   plutonic
precipitate, a substance   typically forms domes, for
greasy luster   it no longer resembles
     fluorite   carborundum

called aquifers   youngest at the top
may form by cooling   resinous and adamantine
     the thickness of a distinguishable
     a hardness greater than 7
     a likeness of the dead

Forgetory: a neologism

How short-sighted
of language
not to endorse
this useful
word: talk
all you like
of *the mental*
faculty of retaining
and recalling past
experience—that's
memory, of course.

This other place:
just as busy.
Chaff heaps high
around the stuff
you wish to summon;
a single minute whisks away
what you were sure
would be indelible
and then forgot.

Tasked

"To copy what's invisible …" ~ W.S. DiPiero

You need your other hand: the one inside
the hand that might hold pen or palette.

You'll need your other eyes, too; not those faded
lamps that want a reading glass for almost any font

these days. No doubt those hazel eyes
recorded things they saw, decade after decade

but what they missed is not accounted for,
and that's what you're after now.

Out of empty space, something formed of lines
and color fills the place: figures, shapes,

an image of wild weather, panoply of an ancient
battleground. Blank, and then blank's opposite:

the canvas fully inhabited. From bare to there
a picture grows out of what hand and eye discern.

You, who can barely draw credible stick figures,
ask words to capture what you cannot see.

Yearning for petrichor

In the sixth year of the drought, dry air grabs each drop almost
before it leaves the watering-can. Conscientious citizens
of our sere state already know the usual garden
is doomed; only pansies in their clay porch pots survive.

In the morning cool, those pansies lift their thoughtful faces
to moisture that steamed yesterday's asparagus, or kale. (Most plants
don't mind grey water, just as a younger sibling used to face,
uncomplaining, the tub after an elder child was bathed.)

Day after long June day, we watch slim strands of cloud
drape themselves across the headlands, then draw back at the sun's
advance. Most of the state bakes crisp. Near the bay, a cooling fog
sweeps back, late in the afternoon, and chases away the heat.

For those of us who have lived elsewhere—in places summer days
might well present a change from bright to rainfall in one quick
blink—this is when we long for the sudden shift: a distant
thunderclap; the speed at which those roiling cumulus approach;

a dash for cover from the drenching gift; but mostly we yearn
for that first, brief moment when the ground responds
with its unforgettable fragrance: earth, stone, and dust applauding
as the first drops of water touch down.

The Moon Sets in a Hurry

Early this morning,
headed for daybreak in Asia
the full, creamy moon plunged out of my
backyard sky. Unhindered by these watchful,
binoculared eyes, briefly bisected by the power-
line, that buttery sphere edged smoothly behind
the protruding eaves of our neighbor's house,
gathered its round self together again, and
in much less time than it has taken
to write these lines, vanished
over the horizon at
a full gallop.

Mortal: a walk to the train

First, the possum
feet-up in the gutter
assuredly not playing;
street trash caught in its claws.

Then, the half-grown Siamese cat
graceful in repose, but far
too still, trail of red drool
connecting mouth and parking-strip.

Last the headlines
screaming of the newest
slaughter of the innocents. Death
toll not final; horror just begun.

And it's an April morning: Bearded
irises exuberant in neighbors'
yards. Sunshine here; house
finch there. A woman walking, weeping.

According to *The Chronicle*'s prediction

Tomorrow morning before dawn
the waning moon aligns itself with Mars.
But sleep still claims me at that hour—
I won't be outside staring at the sky.

Behind the waning moon aligned with Mars
will be the "Beehive" cluster Galileo saw.
I won't be outside, staring at the sky
even though the Great Crab might be visible.

The "Beehive" cluster Galileo saw
was born about 400 million years ago.
It's part of the Great Crab in some celestial way—
(I'm no astronomer; the whole thing baffles me.)

Born just 400 million years ago? a baby still!
Our galaxy is far older than that.
Although I'm no astronomer, the math is easy:
The Milky Way has been here 16 billion years.

But our galaxy is older than most others:
Young Beehive cluster has a lot of company.
Our Milky Way, at 16 billion years of age
has seen 'most everything there is to see.

The Beehive cluster's in good company;
so many of us thought our mornings would last longer
and reckoned we'd see everything there is to see.
Ah well ... why write of what can never be?

Some of us were certain mornings would last forever.
As for me, I'm mostly sleeping at that hour—
That's why I write about what might have been
outside, tomorrow, some time before dawn.

Apartment Living

On the dusty table lie
godetia petals
still of a color between
rouge and burgundy.
They'll fade now they've fallen.

The stalks they fell from
stand, looking
startled, in the vase.
A few more-patient petals
wait their turn.

Anniversary

Do you still start out sleeping
on your side, as if to face me?
Does your cheek
seek my neck nape, your hand
hover empty in the space
where my waist's curve was?

That is what missing you
means to me in my stern exile
one year past parting ways. And this: I want
to turn to you, say
something of little consequence.

When I want a cloudy day

I want it grey so that the lowered clouds backdrop
the many Pantone variations on "spring green."
I want the clouds opaque; their margins
indistinct, with grey sky and bay rolled
together, sans horizon.

I want it bleak and raw.
Slow the dawn down
so that morning creeps along
and scarcely brightens.
I want it dark: dark as the clap-stick
close of your untimely exit from the scene.

When someone I admire dies, even
somebody I never knew, like you,

I want a cloudy day.

How to be spared disappointment

1

Scour the hope jar of its contents
then place it in an airless vault where dark
and cold will keep it empty as a bell
forever.

2

Take a keen look at your future companions;
divide by two
subtract the majority.

3

Pile the kitchen table with promises
made by and to those you love.
Remove the table.

4

This part is the hardest: from first
to last, expect that exhaled breath
will follow inhaled breath and vice versa.

Now stop that.

Extraordinary measures

Now at the downhill end of 91-years young,
my aunt's the oldest baby
in her nursing-home wing. Complete with diaper
and a sippy-cup, she's in a giant
crib with bars to keep her 5 foot 10 inch form
safe from an injudicious tumble.

Until a while ago, the staff would comment brightly,
your aunt sure loves her food—
no problem coaxing her to eat. On my infrequent
visits, we'd share a corner
near the window, stare at one another—
one stare blank, the other sad—while attendants

bustled with the mid-day meal. She'd focus
on the nourishment and slurp, dribbling
quite a lot and sometimes she'd keep chewing
even when the viscous glop was gone. By that time
she couldn't tell you who she was
if her life depended on it, but it didn't.

When I reach her bedside for the final time,
it's clear there is another presence
in the room; the mottled, knotted fingers
of my spectral aunt hardly leave her lap except
to lift an inch or two, defying gravity in clumsy echo
of their former grace, before they fall again,

dry and spotted, incongruous against the pastel
crocheted afghan—a fuzzy thing she would have scorned
when she was still herself. Impossible for me not to study
the parchment temples, which seem to present
the aerial view of a great river system (say, the Amazon,
or, more suitably perhaps, the Ganges) as the veins spider

blue through her skin. She's working hard on her last task—
who really shuffles off this mortal coil? And from the look
in her unblinking eyes you can see she has always
been a hard worker. While in her prime she thoughtfully
elected to decline extraordinary measures;
privately she told me more than once, *do nothing to prolong my life,*

if my mind should die before the rest of me. But I had to do
something to help her, so I made a quick trip
to the mountains, brought back sprigs of fresh
bear clover (*Chamaebatia foliolosa*), waved
the acrid herb beneath her nose. I sang
"like a ship on the water" softly
near the ear where the hearing-aid used to be,
and told her she was free to go
whenever she was ready.

Ten lines of ten syllables each

there is nothing like having to move to
Timbuktu to focus your energy.
okay. that is not where I have to go.
but to have to move is to have to think
of all endings—yes, even the big one.
every death in your life will resurface.
when you think about where you have to go
you wonder, how will the new home differ?
will there be a place for your easy chair?
can you take the little rosebush with you?

A Return

"Curtsey while you're thinking what to say. It saves time."
~ Lewis Carroll

Lie to the weather. Tell the calendar off.
Coax brittle boxes to disclose their history
and then discard it all. Be spacious now.

Argue with the Fates. They'll always win
the final round, but you may balk them briefly.
Seize the day despite its wriggling.

Fall in love with something—anything—
to shift the weight that cumbers you.
Your heart. It isn't empty. Listen.

Like Goldilocks

or some other fussy character
from an olden book
thick with tales of fairies and trolls

the mockingbird outside my window
in the heavy-laden loquat tree must peck
a single taste from one yellow globe

and then another, then a third, before
knowing which is sweetest
and best for her delectation

by which time the memory of the first
loquat is lost, and another branch beckons
and Uh-oh, here's another bird, bent

on the same pursuit, aimed
for the very piece of fruit
you had your eye on—the perfect

exemplar, the one the gods
themselves were waiting
to pick, but it's too late now:

brief clash of the birds,
feathers flashing as they leap
and accost each other

knocking the drupe from its stem
in their combat and then
off they fly, because, fallen,

the object of their desire
becomes just one slightly
too-soft loquat soon

to be a feast
for the ants
on the ground.

One ascent of Mount Vision

If only it were all
uphill from here—
the ground always rising
to meet my feet; each step a slap
at gravity's vanity.

And the steady filling
of the chest
with air—that's the body in business:
aerobic respiration;
nucleotides hard at work.

See, uphill allows the heart
to show its mettle
as muscle (sturdy pump
goes gladly to the well
    the well
      the well)
this lovely pounding—
bone skull
amplifies the sound
to a drum solo in my ear.

And the sea-level poison
pours out, drop by slippery
steaming drop
to drench my grey bandanna.

Please, tell me
I need not descend
skitter-foot over rocks and dirt
momentum
like a pushy foe who tries
to chivvy me to the precipice.

Let me continue this steady
climb, angles of afternoon light in my face
the sought object still simple:
invisible
because it is too near.

Notes to the epigraphs, titles, subject matter

Contemporary students of poetry reckon Ezra Pound opened up a giant can of worms for future poets with the three words I quote in this epigraph, but in fact the injunction antedated him by about 3500 years, if it is true that Ch'engT'ang had the words inscribed on his wash-basin. (Chiding the muse)

The title of this poem is the final line of Elizabeth Bishop's poem, "Filling Station." ("Somebody loves us all")

The quoted lines in the epigraph come from *The Hidden Reality* (Knopf, 2011) by Brian Greene. (Parallel lines)

I had occasion to study a list of job titles issued by the state government, and was bemused at the number of occupations I had never heard of. (Odd: Job)

In 2001, I spotted the epigraph on a bumper-sticker on a car parked in my neighborhood. I have never seen the bumper-sticker again since. (The garden came first)

Here, the epigraph is a line from Bishop's poem, "Sestina." (Grow Sorrow)

Dealing with the nine-headed Hydra was Hercules's second labor; he still had 10 more to face. But he could not have triumphed over Hydra without help; I would like to see him tackle *oxalis pes-caprae* by himself. (Hydra of the many names)

The lines quoted in the epigraph are from E.M. Forster's novel, *Howards End*. As for the paradox, Zeno propounded several, but I am thinking of the dichotomy paradox. (Vinculum)

The title is taken from Emily Dickinson's poem numbered 1755 in the Thomas Johnson collection of her complete poems; the italicized phrase is from the poem numbered 341 in that volume. I am forever in Dickinson's debt, as I am to Gerard Manley Hopkins. (If bees are few)

The statement I quote in the epigraph does not appear in *Bartlett's Quotations*, but I have heard it opined in several languages throughout my life. (Stuck/torn)

The epigraph is a passage from Jonathan Culler's work on the linguist, Ferdinand de Saussure. (Sonnet for constituents not permitted)

"Here be dragons" is a notation used in medieval cartography to indicate uncharted waters. (*Hic sunt dracones*)

The italicized phrases are all from Hopkins's poem, "God's Grandeur," which has saved my life many times over. (I mumble *deo gratias*)

Pappus of Alexandria was a mathematician, but this passage about the selective "knowledge" of bees struck me profoundly, and led to the writing of the poem. (In theory)

The title is a line from the poem "Twelfth morning; or What You will," by Elizabeth Bishop. The line captured my fancy, and I wanted to see where it might take me. ("The sea's off somewhere, doing nothing")

A while back, I needed accurate information on the speed of light, and happened upon a website from the University of Cambridge, which provided me with the title (and impetus) for this poem. ("Light travels at 300,000 kilometres per second."

In a chapter titled "The sense of time" from his *Psychology: the Briefer Course* William James begins by saying "The sensible present has duration," but then proceeds to ask the question I quote in the epigraph. (Present: Three Takes)

In Act 1, scene VII of Macbeth, Shakespeare refers to memory as "warder of the brain." (The warder of his brain)

The pieces of this found poem were all lifted from a handout titled "Rocks and Minerals" (written by Prof. John Harris at Mills College for a class on California Natural History.) ("do not look directly into the light")

The epigraph is a phrase from Di Piero's poem, "On a Picture by Cézanne," published in *Poetry* magazine. (Tasked)

I am older than the word "petrichor," but I have loved it ever since I heard it for the first time. (Yearning for petrichor)

My learning of the death of Seamus Heaney prompted this one. (When I want a cloudy day)

The excellent advice given by the Red Queen to Alice in Lewis Carroll's *Through the Looking-glass* is rarely heeded nowadays, mainly because most of us never see any need to curtsey. (A return)

Mount Vision (elev. 1,282) is located in Point Reyes National Seashore. (One ascent of Mount Vision)

Acknowledgements

I am grateful to the journals, print or online, in which the following poems first appeared, some in slightly different form or with a different title:

Ambit: "All of it, and spring as well"
Blue Lyra Review: "Posture: [im]Perfect"
Catamaran Literary Reader: "One ascent of Mount Vision"
Center: A Journal of the Literary Arts: "To measure the dark"
Eclectica: "The Ache of Lack"
Kestrel: "When I want a cloudy day"
Lunch Ticket: "Walking in Lines with Five Feet"
Mason's Road: "The warder of his brain"
New Millennium Writings: "*Hic sunt dracones*"
Peacock Journal: "Seasoned;" "Cronos: his tempo;"
    "Provenance, as applied to a stone"
Pirene's Fountain: "Chiding the muse"
Quiddity: "Sisyphus addresses his boon companion;"
    "The garden came first"
Rat's Ass Review: "Truth or Dare;" "A brief natural history
    of the sub-continent;" "Anniversary"
Right Hand Pointing: "On witnessing the descent of
    Another into Depression"
Rose Red Review: "I leave the Iron Age entirely to one side"
Syn/aes/the/tic: "Sonnet for Constituents Not Permitted"
The American Journal of Poetry: "Somebody loves us all;"
    "Hear that lonesome whistle blow"
The Café Review: "Cassandra talks in her sleep;" "Stuck/torn"
The Lake: "But we are really the dust of ancient stars;"
    "How to be spared disappointment"
Turtle Island Quarterly: "Diorama, minus one dimension"
Unsplendid: "Ten lines of ten syllables each"
Whale Road Review: "Late summer, lasting"
Where Icarus Falls, Santa Barbara Review Publications:
    "Litany"

Both of my late parents loved poetry, and they set my feet on the path of loving it as well. It is my good fortune to have supportive siblings, and even my nieces, nephews, and cousins have encouraged me to persevere with the manuscript that became this book. Classmates and faculty from my years at Mills College have buoyed me during the thirty years it has taken to accumulate a body of work that belongs between the covers of a book. Robin Wells, Merle Bachman, Dorianne Laux, Cynthia Imperatore, Stephen Ratcliffe, Diana O'Hehir, Marilyn Chandler McEntyre, and the late Chana Bloch: this means you. (I was an undergraduate and a graduate student at Mills long before the changes in direction that have recently taken place. I deplore the current administration's decision to terminate tenured faculty.) ~ A vehement thank-you to Robin Stratton at Big Table, for turning a long chorus of No into the blessed Yes, and then for amazing patience in working with me on turning a manuscript into this book. I couldn't have asked for a more perfect image for the front cover, graciously provided by the people at the Richard Diebenkorn Foundation. And a host of colleagues and friends over the years have supported my dogged preoccupation with poetry—you *are* too many to name, and I hope you know who you are. But in the final category are three women who constitute the *sine qua non* of this book: members of my poetry group who started seeing versions of some of these poems as long ago as 2001. Katherine Case, Patricia Caspers, and Jennifer K. Sweeney put forth effort far beyond my wild dreams. I cannot possibly thank you enough, though I will keep trying.